PEYTON MANNING

PEYTON MANNING

Precision Passer

Jeff Savage

LERNER **SPORTS**
AN IMPRINT OF LERNER PUBLISHING GROUP

For Bailey Conroy Savage—my son and hero

This book is available in two editions:
Library binding by LernerSports
Soft cover by First Avenue Editions
Imprints of Lerner Publishing Group
241 First Avenue North
Minneapolis, MN 55401 U.S.A.

Website address: www.lernerbooks.com

Library of Congress Cataloging-in-Publication Data

Savage, Jeff, 1961–
 Peyton Manning : precision passer / by Jeff Savage.
  p. cm.
 Includes bibliographical references and index.
 ISBN: 0–8225–3683–8 (lib. bdg. : alk. paper)
 ISBN: 0–8225–9865–5 (pbk : alk. paper)
 1. Manning, Peyton—Juvenile literature. 2. Football
players—United States—Biography—Juvenile literature.
[1. Manning, Peyton. 2. Football players.] I. Title.
GV939.M289 S28 2001
796.332'092–dc21   2001001690

Manufactured in the United States of America
1 2 3 4 5 6 – JR – 06 05 04 03 02 01

Contents

The Real Thing

Peyton Manning had a funny feeling as he prepared his team for action. He leaned into the huddle and told his linemen, "Hey, give me an extra second here. I might take a shot down the field." Peyton stepped to the **line of scrimmage** in his blue jersey with the white number 18, the same number his father had worn for the New Orleans Saints a generation earlier.

Outside the RCA Dome in Indianapolis, Indiana, a cold rain fell. Inside, a sellout crowd of 56,816 had come to see their beloved Colts battle the Jacksonville Jaguars. Millions of other Americans watched the *Monday Night Football* game on television.

The season before, the Jaguars had allowed the fewest points in the National Football League and had posted the league's best record. One week earlier in this 2000 season, the five-year-old franchise had recorded its first shutout in team history. What's more, they had played five *Monday Night Football* games and had won them all. This was Peyton's first *Monday Night Football* game. Would he feel the pressure?

Peyton has a favorite quote, the words of Pro Football Hall of Fame coach Chuck Noll: "Pressure is something you feel only when you don't know what you're doing." But Peyton knew exactly what he was doing that night. One play earlier, on his first throw of the game, he had whip-cracked a pass to Terrence Wilkins for a 12-yard gain. Now, preparing for the **snap** once again, Peyton saw what he had suspected—the Jaguars move into a tighter **coverage.** He put his hand to his side and gave a secret signal to wide receiver Marvin Harrison, changing the play. Instead of a **curl route,** Harrison would run a **post pattern.**

Peyton took the snap and faked a handoff to Edgerrin James. The **play-action** fooled the defense for a split second. Peyton dropped back to pass.

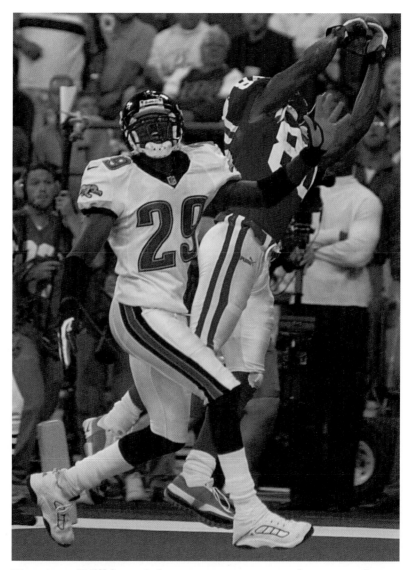

Terrence Wilkins, right, ***attempts to catch a pass from Peyton.***

Defenders came at him. Just as he was about to be swallowed by the **pass rush,** he stepped and let the ball fly. Harrison was sprinting ahead of defender Aaron Beasley by a stride. Peyton's pass arched through the air like a rainbow. It came down, down, down, and into Harrison's arms on the fly. Beasley dived and missed. Harrison galloped into the end zone for a touchdown. The play covered 76 yards, and the fans came to their feet roaring. The national television audience had just seen why Peyton Manning is considered one of the game's best quarterbacks.

Peyton has a boyish face. But his intensity shows in his eyes. At the line of scrimmage, his eyes are wide. They don't blink. His pupils dart from side to side, examining the defensive coverage. His brain whirs, thinking through the team playbook in seconds. If he decides to change the play, he stamps his foot, snaps his fingers, claps his hands, puts his fist on his hip, or waves to signal his teammates.

"Peyton, he's like a computer," said teammate James. "It's like he's thinking of 100 plays at one time." Quarterback coach Bruce Arians adds, "It's like I'm coaching a piranha. He eats [all the information] you give him and wants more."

Peyton is both a smart player and a physcially fit athlete.

Peyton's intelligence isn't the only thing that makes him a great quarterback. He has all the physical tools. He weighs 230 pounds, stands six-feet, five-inches tall, and sees easily downfield. He has a quick-fire release that helps him avoid getting sacked. He throws with zip and pop and keen accuracy. He has great poise and football instincts. He makes all the right moves.

For instance, after Peyton's bomb to Marvin Harrison for the score, the Jaguars responded by **double-teaming** Harrison. Peyton simply found other holes in Jacksonville's coverage. He threw to different receivers and soon had completed seven straight passes for 126 yards. "If they double-team Marvin, we can beat them with other guys," said Peyton. "We have other weapons on offense." Indianapolis's main weapon, of course, is Peyton.

The Jaguars tied the game at 7 on a pass from Mark Brunell to Jimmy Smith midway through the second quarter. But Peyton grabbed the lead right back. On third-and-eleven from the Jacksonville 27, he **dropped back,** dodged the rush, and fired a pass down the middle of the field. The ball sailed inside the five-yard line, right into the hands of streaking Terrence Wilkins for the touchdown. On the

Colts' next possession, Peyton whisked his team 72 yards in four plays for another score.

The Jaguars did not give up. They scored another touchdown to bring the game to 21–14. Then Peyton seized control for good. He led the Colts on four scoring drives in the second half. With a pair of field goals, two touchdowns, and a safety, the Colts won in a 43–14 blowout.

For the game, Peyton had completed 23 of 36 passes for a team record of 440 yards. This was his second time passing for more than 400 yards in just over two years in the NFL. Johnny Unitas, who quarterbacked the Colts from 1956 to 1972, is often called the greatest pure passer in NFL history. Yet Unitas threw for over 400 yards just once in his celebrated career.

Wilkins was quick to praise Peyton after the victory over the Jaguars. "Whatever they tried on defense, Peyton had an answer for it," he said. "The big players come up big in the big games. This was a huge game for us, and Peyton couldn't have been any bigger."

Legendary quarterback Y. A. Tittle, a Hall of Famer from the '40s, '50s, and '60s, summed up the feelings of many when he marveled, "That Manning boy, he's the real thing."

Born to Throw

Growing up as the son of an NFL quarterback might seem glamorous, and in many ways it was. But for Peyton Manning, it was difficult, too. "People watch your every move," he said. "Some people almost hope for you to mess up." Because the media spotlight shone brightly on the Manning family, Peyton went through childhood taking careful steps.

Peyton's father, Archie *(pictured on facing page)*, was a clean-cut, redheaded **All-American** quarterback. He had restored the University of Mississippi's football program to supremacy before playing fourteen years in the NFL. Peyton's mother, Olivia, was a homecoming queen at Mississippi ("Ole Miss").

Archie and Olivia married in 1971, the same year Archie graduated and turned pro.

Archie signed on with the sad-sack New Orleans Saints. He was a smart, scrambling quarterback, but the team played poorly. In Archie's eleven seasons

Peyton used to watch his father play in the Superdome, home of the New Orleans Saints.

with the Saints, they never had a winning record. In the stands, fans sometimes wore brown paper bags over their heads out of embarrassment. They called their team "the Aints."

Archie had been with the Saints for four years when Peyton Williams Manning was born on March 24, 1976. Peyton was the second of Archie and Olivia's three sons. Cooper had been born two years earlier, and Eli was born four years later. The boys grew up in a big yellow house in the sycamore-lined Garden District of New Orleans, Louisiana.

Peyton loved sports right from the start. By age three, he was playing football with his father and Cooper in the living room. Using a miniature football, Archie would try to get past his boys on his knees. By age four, Peyton was performing a seven-step drop back and throwing a Nerf football across the living room. His long fingers helped him grip the ball. "He was a chunky boy with huge hands," recalled his kindergarten teacher, Laurie Diamond. Each Christmas, Peyton, Cooper, and Eli found gifts of pads, jerseys, and other football gear beneath the tree.

Peyton and his brothers often went to Saints games at the Superdome in New Orleans. They got to romp on the field during halftime and go into the locker room after games. Not knowing any better, Peyton and Cooper once asked their father if they could wear paper bags on their heads like the other Saints fans, because they thought the bags were "cool." Another time, when the home fans were booing Archie and his losing team, Peyton's mother turned around to see her sons joining in. "Boo! Boo, Archie! Boo!" they yelled.

The truth was, Archie was a fine quarterback and an even better father. "There were a lot of days when he got beat up on the field and the Saints lost badly," said Peyton, "but he signed every autograph, he did every single interview, and that's what it's all about. He never brought his sorrows home, either. When he came home to the family, you'd thought that he'd just won the Super Bowl."

Even though the Saints weren't winners, Peyton knew that his dad had once been a hero. During eighth grade, he would lie awake at night listening to tapes of Archie's college games at Mississippi. He listened to the tapes over and over, memorizing the names of the players, memorizing the words of the announcer: "Manning brings 'em to the line. Manning sprints out right, throws . . . touchdown! Touchdown, Ole Miss! On a pass from Archie Manning!"

Peyton, left, **_always wanted to live up to the Mississippi football legacy of his father,_** right.

He would hear the cheers and throw his hands in the air. He would try to feel what his dad had felt. He dreamed of being a college quarterback hero, just like his dad.

Peyton was determined to do well at everything. At the Isidore Newman School, which he attended from kindergarten through high school, he was intent on making good grades. Peyton worked hard to be a quarterback, too. He loved throwing passes to Cooper, Eli, and neighborhood friends, and they would play catch for hours. Cooper was a great pass receiver and runner. Eli wanted to be a quarterback, just like Archie and Peyton.

In the fall of 1991, during his sophomore year in high school, Peyton became the starting quarterback for the varsity football team. Cooper, then a senior, was a gifted wide receiver on the team. Peyton and Cooper played their one season of football together that year. "That year made us buddies," Cooper said. Together, they set school records and led their team all the way to the state semifinals.

Unknown to the coaches and other players, the brothers had devised their own set of secret hand signals. "If I touched my nose, it was a come-back pass—to Cooper, naturally. Tap my helmet and it was a curl," said Peyton. "It wasn't exactly fair to the other receivers, I admit, but they didn't know, and it was working, and we were winning, so we kept doing it." Only the boys' father knew about their system.

The duo accounted for 73 completions, 1,250 yards, and 13 touchdowns during the 1991 season. Newman went 12–1 that year before losing to mighty Haynesville High, 27–21. The loss came when Peyton threw an interception with thirty seconds left in the game. As the team left the field, Cooper put his arm around his little brother and told him not to worry: They would have a chance to win a title together again in two years.

Cooper had won a scholarship to play wide receiver for Ole Miss. College recruiters were already sending letters to Peyton, too. Coach Bobby Bowden of Florida State had even sent a handwritten note. But Peyton had already made up his mind. He would go to Mississippi to play with his brother— to be like his dad. That was the plan.

The plan did not work. Cooper never played a game at Ole Miss. Several months before school started, his right hand went numb. Then the numbness spread to his leg. Cooper finally told his family that something was wrong. Doctors discovered that he was suffering from spinal stenosis, a condition that threatened to paralyze him.

Cooper underwent surgery to treat his illness. Before the surgery, he wrote Peyton a letter. It said, in part, "I would like to live my dream of playing football through you. Although I cannot play anymore, I know I can still get the same feeling out of watching my little brother do what he does best. I love you, Peyt, and only great things [lie] ahead for you. Thanks for everything on and off the field." The surgery helped Cooper, but he could not play sports like before. His football career was suddenly over.

Peyton struggled to cope with his brother's illness. "It was real tough for me," he said, "because I knew how hard it was for Cooper." Eventually, Peyton gained a perspective on football and life. "I take every practice now as my last one. Any play could be my last, so I try my best on every one," he says. "And more than that, Cooper's condition taught me to appreciate life and to realize, hey, there's more to life than football."

Peyton flourished during his last two years on the Newman School football field. Newman went 11−2 in Peyton's junior year. During his senior year, the team went 10−0 in the regular season, and Peyton racked up 39 touchdowns. The Touchdown Club of Columbus, Ohio—an organization that had twice named Archie College Player of the Year—called Peyton the top offensive high school player in the

Cooper Manning can no longer play football but enjoys watching Peyton on the field.

nation. In Peyton's three years as a starter, he had led Newman to a 34—5 record and had thrown for 7,207 yards and 92 touchdowns.

Major universities clamored for him to sign with them. Archie didn't want to push Peyton into a football career, and he never meddled in any way. "I distanced myself from the football part of it," said Archie. "There is nothing worse than a daddy interfering with a high school coaching staff. It was the same during college recruiting. Peyton could have gone anywhere. All I told him was 'I'm here for you, but you make the call.'"

Although Peyton had originally planned to play for Ole Miss, he still considered offers from other colleges. He finally narrowed his choices to two: Ole Miss and the University of Tennessee. Then he made his decision: Tennessee.

Immediately, angry Mississippians bombarded Peyton and his family with cruel phone calls and letters. The fans felt that Peyton had betrayed them. Peyton did not see it that way. "I was just mad I couldn't go to both places at once," he said. "It's really too bad it had to come down to one."

Peyton gave several reasons for his decision. During recruiting visits, he had bonded with the Tennessee coaches. Also, as much as he wanted to walk in his father's footsteps at Mississippi, he did not want special treatment. "I didn't want to go where I would become an instant celebrity without ever taking a snap," he said.

Finally, Peyton's dream of playing with his brother Cooper had been dashed. He would later describe his fantasy: "We're both in Ole Miss uniforms, gray and red," he said. "I picture how it would have been. He comes into my dream, catching a pass. Then he throws the ball up into the stands . . . Touchdown, Ole Miss!"

Losing that dream was too painful, and Peyton needed to move away from it. "I have no doubt I'd have gone to Ole Miss if Cooper hadn't gotten sick," he said. "Cooper's illness took the shine off."

Instead, Peyton transferred his football dreams to the University of Tennessee Volunteers.

Instead of going to Mississippi, Peyton put on the orange-and-white jersey of the Tennessee Volunteers.

Volunteering
for Duty

Game day at the University of Tennessee is like a statewide celebration. The school's Neyland Stadium fills up with more than 100,000 fans, many dressed in the team's colors: orange and white. The stadium sits on the banks of the Tennessee River in Knoxville, so many fans come to the game by boat. Parties along the river start before the game and go long into the night. "Playing here is so special," said Peyton. "I love the tradition, the fans, the whole scene."

Peyton arrived in Knoxville six weeks early so he could work out with the upperclassmen. "He came in with an attitude that I've never seen in any freshman," said senior fullback Eric Lane. Peyton was third or fourth string on the quarterback depth chart, behind Jerry Colquitt and Todd Helton and tied with another freshman, Branndon Stewart. It didn't appear that Peyton would play as a freshman, but he wanted to be ready—just in case. His chance came sooner than expected.

The Volunteers played their 1994 season opener against UCLA in Los Angeles, California. Three minutes into the game, senior starter Colquitt suffered a knee injury, which ended his season. Junior backup Helton replaced him but was ineffective. With Tennessee trailing 18—0 late in the second quarter, coach Phillip Fulmer turned toward the team's bench and reached for Peyton. A chance to play so soon? Was this a dream?

Peyton ran onto the field and huddled up with his teammates. He told them not to worry—that even though he was a freshman, he could do the job. He said it was time to focus, time to rally, time to . . . "We've been here three years!" lineman Jason Layman interrupted. "We know what to do. Shut up and call the play!"

Peyton handed off three straight times, and on fourth down the Volunteers punted. Peyton took a seat back on the bench for the rest of the game. Still, his moment on the field was important to him. "I was happy they put me in after Helton," he said. "That meant a lot to me, that they now consider me the Number 2 guy."

Three weeks later, Peyton was number one. In the fourth game of the season, against Mississippi State, Todd Helton went down with a season-ending knee injury. Peyton was summoned off the bench for good. He threw a 76-yard touchdown pass to Kendrick Jones to rally the Vols, but they fell short in that game, losing 24—21.

One week later, Peyton made his first college start against the seventeenth-ranked Washington State Cougars. They were 3—0 and had not allowed a touchdown all season. Tennessee's game plan was to be careful with the football—throw less to avoid interceptions. "You've got to avoid losing before you can win," Coach Fulmer told Peyton.

Peyton threw just 14 passes in the game and completed half of them for 79 yards. One long pass, a 41-yard completion to Jones, put Tennessee in position for the winning score. "It felt good to let it loose once," said Peyton about the throw. The Volunteers won in a squeaker, 10—9. Most important, Peyton did not commit a **turnover** in the game.

By November, Peyton was comfortable running the offense. For the season, he completed over 60 percent of his passes for 11 touchdowns and just six interceptions. The Vols went 7–1 with him as a starter. He capped the season with a stirring performance in the Gator Bowl. He hit 12 of 19 passes for 189 yards and broke loose for a 29-yard run to spark Tennessee to a 45–23 win over Virginia Tech. He was an easy choice to be named Southeastern Conference Freshman of the Year.

Peyton was also a serious student. He took difficult courses such as calculus and maintained good grades. He also made time for a girlfriend, Ashley Thompson. They had met at a party on campus, but Ashley wasn't exactly impressed at first. "He was wearing this really ugly pastel shirt," she said, "and I had a feeling he was going to be a nerd." Ashley reluctantly agreed to go on a date with him later that year. Peyton impressed her with his manners. He pulled out her chair at the restaurant and opened doors for her.

When Peyton wasn't spending time with Ashley or doing his homework, he was holed up in his bedroom studying the Volunteers playbook. His apartment mates called him "Caveman" and his room "the

Cave." On Saturday night after a home game, while his teammates were out celebrating, Peyton sat in his room studying videotapes of the game.

He also spent a lot of time in the Tennessee film room, examining films of opposing defenses. Reporters often phoned the film room late at night in search of a coach, and Peyton answered instead. Tennessee's offensive coordinator, Dave Cutcliffe, had to do extra studying himself just to keep up with the young quarterback. "He always has a bunch of questions," Cutcliffe explained. "He's somebody very special, and I don't want to let him down."

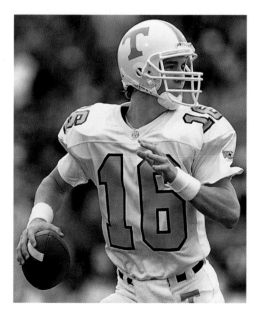

Peyton drops back for a pass in 1995.

A victorious Peyton on the phone after beating Alabama 41—14

Peyton's hard work paid off. The Volunteers rolled impressively through the 1995 season. They carved up Arkansas in a 49—31 victory and destroyed Alabama in a 41—14 rout. The team's lone loss of the season was to Florida on a rainy day in Gainesville. Peyton had guided the Vols to an early 30—14 lead in a drizzle. But then the skies opened up, and the Gators rained touchdowns on the helpless Vol defense. The result was a 62–37 drubbing. Peyton left the field discouraged. In the tunnel outside the locker room, he met his father. "We're proud of you," Archie whispered.

Peyton was becoming popular around Knoxville, although he tried to downplay his fame. "People build me up too much," he said. "My dad was an All-America. I'm just a clumsy sophomore. I'm pretty much an average guy." Opponents disagreed. Peyton

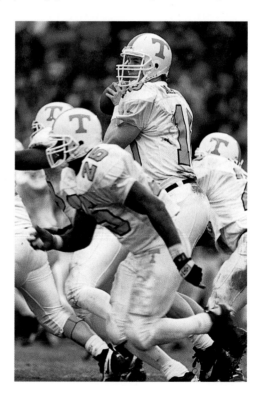

Peyton and the Volunteers played hard against Kentucky and won 34–31.

bewildered defenses and set new team records, including most completions and yards in a season. But he was careful with the ball. He threw 380 passes and just four interceptions, an NCAA record for the lowest interception rate in a season. With a victory over Ohio State in the Citrus Bowl, Tennessee finished the season ranked third in the country.

Many athletes who achieve success tend to relax and level out. But Peyton set his sights high. A few days after the bowl victory over Ohio State, he was already calling wide receivers and defensive backs, trying to organize informal practices. "It was tough for me, adjusting to his work ethic," said receiver Joey Kent.

The following month, in February, Peyton attended the Davey O'Brien Award banquet in Fort Worth, Texas. The award is given annually to the top college quarterback. Peyton had been runner-up for the award, finishing behind Florida's Danny Wuerffel. But he attended the banquet anyway. He knew several NFL quarterbacks would be there. At the reception, he sought advice about quarterbacking from Ty Detmer, Kerry Collins, Steve Young, and others. "I figured I had two hours with those guys," said Peyton. "I wasn't going to waste it by making small talk."

Each spring, NFL scouts visit college campuses to scope out seniors for the upcoming NFL draft. Peyton would not be part of the draft, because he was just a sophomore, but he awed the pro scouts. New York Giants scout Tom Boisture voiced the opinion of many when he said, "He's the first pick. Last year, this year, next year, whenever he wants."

Peyton's junior season was marked by another heartbreaking defeat to rival Florida. Before a record crowd at Neyland Stadium, the Gators stormed out to a 35–0 lead less than five minutes into the second quarter. Peyton rallied his team. He set school records with 37 completions in 65 attempts for 492 yards. But the Volunteers fell short, losing the game 35–29.

The loss did not slow Peyton's rise. He became the first Tennessee quarterback to throw for more than 3,000 yards in a season. The Volunteers finished the season 10–2, including a 48–28 victory over Northwestern in the Citrus Bowl. After three seasons, Peyton held nineteen school records and a 28–4 win-loss record.

He became a statewide hero, just like his father had been in Mississippi. When people spotted him at restaurants or malls, they chanted his name.

Dozens of Tennessee families named their babies Peyton and sent photos to him at the team office. Knoxville named a street Peyton Manning Pass, and the Knoxville Zoo even named a baby giraffe after him. But Peyton became so uncomfortable with the attention that he hid in public. "I tried disguises," he said. "Shades, hats—but they always spotted me."

During Peyton's junior year, rumors swirled that he would leave Tennessee for the NFL. He had already completed enough credits to graduate. He almost certainly would be chosen first overall in the draft. At the Citrus Bowl, a deafening chant had filled the stadium: "One more year! One more year!" The fans begged their hero to stay, but the allure of pro riches was great.

On March 5, 1997, Peyton called a press conference. He had made his decision: He was staying at Tennessee. He had already finished his undergraduate class work, with a major in speech communication and a 3.61 grade-point average. He said that he would play his senior season while taking graduate-level classes in sports management.

The decision was not easy for Peyton. "I'm human. The $25 million, $30 million, believe me, I looked at the money," he said. "But remaining a college

Head coach Phillip Fulmer gives Peyton a few pointers before sending him onto the field.

student was strongest in my heart." NFL coaches applauded Peyton's decision. They called it refreshing. The happiest coach of all was Tennessee's Phillip Fulmer. "When Peyton made his announcement," said Fulmer, "I felt the earth shake." He continued, "You can talk about Peyton for hours, and it sounds like some fairy tale."

Not all fairy tales have perfect endings. The Volunteers went 11–1 the next year, losing to Florida again in the regular season and losing to Nebraska in the Orange Bowl. But Peyton was clearly the nation's best college quarterback. He threw for 36 touchdowns and 3,819 yards, including a record-breaking 523 yards in a game against Kentucky. He threw five touchdown passes in two games and four touchdowns in three others.

More important, Peyton had a blast that season. He enjoyed weekly chicken-wing dinners with his offensive linemen. He was a groomsman in team-mate Marcus Nash's wedding. After games, he joined family and friends outside the stadium for parties. Once, when he saw students camped out overnight, waiting to buy tickets for a game, he bought twenty pizzas for them.

Peyton received the ultimate collegiate honor in February 1998, when he won the Sullivan Award, given each year to the nation's top amateur athlete. He was flattered and grateful. But individual awards were unimportant to him. "College is supposed to be the best four years of your life," he said. "I made a lot of friends. I created a bunch of memories. These are the times that will stay with me.

Peyton celebrates after a 17–10 win over Vanderbilt.

You can talk about the awards, but that isn't what's important."

It was hard for Peyton to leave Tennessee. It was even harder for the Volunteers to say good-bye. "Peyton has the brains of a lawyer, the heart of a warrior, and the soul of a gentleman," said Carmen Tegano, an associate athletic director at Tennessee. "I won't see another kid like him. I hope I do, but I know I won't.

Ryan Leaf, left, *and Peyton Manning at the 1998 NFL draft in New York City*

All-Pro in the Making

Peyton and Washington State quarterback Ryan Leaf were sure to be the first two players taken in the 1998 NFL draft. The only question was—who would be picked first?

The Indianapolis Colts had the first choice in 1998. Team owner Jim Irsay met Peyton for breakfast one day to get to know him. The conversation went well, and they said good-bye in the parking lot. As Manning walked toward his car, he realized he wanted Irsay to know one more thing about him. He spun around and called out. He looked Irsay in the eye. "I'll win for you," he said. Irsay was startled—and impressed. "It sent a shiver up my spine," Irsay said.

Jim Irsay, left, ***the owner of the Indianapolis Colts, with new draft pick Peyton Manning***

At the draft, the Colts wasted no time turning in their selection card. It read: Peyton Manning. "Peyton was excited about being a Colt," said Irsay. "He wanted us to pick him." The trouble was, the Colts were a losing team. They had managed just 3 wins in 16 games the year before. Could Peyton handle losing? Those who knew him well had no doubt. "Peyton is talented," said one pro scout. "He'll handle the inferno of going to a 3–13 team. He's a sure player."

The Colts had some other good players. Marshall Faulk was a hard-to-catch running back. Marvin Harrison was a fleet receiver. Ken Dilger was a sturdy tight end. There was hope. "I realize what I'm getting into," said Peyton. "It's exciting to be part of a rebuilding process. It's a challenge."

The Colts offered Peyton $48 million to play for them for six years. Naturally, he agreed. He also signed contracts for millions more, agreeing to **endorse** products and services for a credit card company, a phone company, a shoe company, and an electronics company. His new Colts teammates gave him a nickname the first day of practice. They called him PowerBall, after the lottery game, because he was suddenly so rich. Peyton laughed. He knew just what to do with all the extra money. He soon formed an organization called the PeyBack Foundation that would give money to people in need.

When Peyton joined the team, he asked that his locker be placed with the lockers of the offensive

Peyton gets sacked by Miami Dolphins linebacker Derrick Rodgers during his first NFL game.

linemen, the men who protected him on the field. Some quarterbacks stay separate. They want to be treated as superior to the other players. But Peyton wanted to be just one of the guys. He became fast friends with his linemen. "Peyton is down-to-earth and treats everyone with respect," said left tackle Tarik Glenn.

Most rookie quarterbacks don't play during their first season. The few who do struggle. But the Colts knew that Peyton was their future, so they put him at the line of scrimmage at the first practice and kept him there. As expected, he struggled.

In his NFL debut, in the RCA Dome against the visiting Miami Dolphins, he completed 21 of 37 passes for 302 yards, which was stellar. But he also threw three interceptions, including one that was re-turned for a game-clinching touchdown. The Colts lost the game 24—15. "I made some mistakes," said Peyton afterward. "Hopefully I'll learn from them."

Peyton threw three more interceptions the next week against the New England Patriots. After five weeks, he had racked up 12 interceptions and just four touchdowns. At least the Colts finally won a game, though. After starting 0—4, they beat Ryan Leaf's San Diego Chargers 17—12.

Peyton wasn't panicking just yet. "Sure, the pro game is faster than the college level, and more complex," he said. "But experience is your best teacher. I will learn, but it will take some time. This is not a sprint, it's a marathon." Despite four more losses, coach Jim Mora said, "Peyton is making great progress, he really is."

As the weeks went by, Indianapolis fans grew to appreciate Peyton for his kindness, generosity, and determination to help build a winner. By the season's midpoint, he already had three offers to host his own radio and TV shows. He declined the offers. Every minute of his time was already accounted for.

Each day before practice, Peyton spent several hours in the Colts' film room studying videotapes of opposing defenses. At practice, the Colts had to adjust their drills so that Peyton could keep throwing the ball while the receivers rested. "I have to make sure he doesn't wear out our receivers," said quarterback coach Bruce Arians. After practice ended and the other players headed to the showers, Peyton stayed on the field—to run sprints. Then he went to the weight room to pump iron. At night in his apartment, he memorized the team's playbook—not just the plays involving his position but every play in the book.

Peyton works very hard in the Colts training camp.

47

Peyton also made time for speaking engagements, signing autographs, and visiting schools. He even took time out to see his younger brother, Eli, play football. Eli by then was a senior quarterback for Newman High. (Two years later, Eli would live out Peyton's dream and play quarterback for Ole Miss.)

The Colts finished the season 3–13 again. But Peyton set a slew of team and league records to cap what the league called "the finest rookie season in NFL history." Among his top marks were Colts and NFL rookie records in completions, attempts, yards, and touchdowns. The Colts weren't winners, but no matter how bad things got, Peyton hung in there. In fact, he was the only quarterback in the NFL to play every down that season. "It was frustrating and disappointing," he said. "But you can either sit there and feel sorry for yourself or learn from it and do something about it."

Peyton believed that the Colts were on the verge of breaking through. "It's going to happen," he said. "It's just a matter of when." The breakthrough happened the next season. First, the team traded Marshall Faulk to the Saint Louis Rams for a high draft pick. They used the pick to draft running back Edgerrin James. "I enjoyed the year I got to play

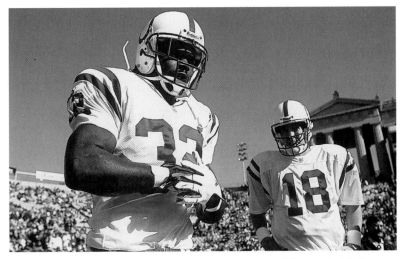

Edgerrin James, left, ***and Peyton on Soldier Field for a game against the Chicago Bears***

with Marshall," said Peyton. "But I'm glad to be playing with Edgerrin. He has the power to pop it inside or take it outside. Hopefully, he and I can play together for a long time."

Next, Peyton became more of a team leader. For instance, if a receiver dropped a pass in practice, he let it be known that such mistakes could not happen in games. He was not bossy. He was firm, but fair. "My rookie year I didn't take control as much," he admitted. "I was a little bit more reserved. You want to earn the respect of your teammates before you start barking orders."

Peyton barked orders in 1999, and his teammates gladly marched because they trusted him. The difference was clear from the start. In week two against the New England Patriots, Peyton hooked up with Marvin Harrison for three first-half touchdowns. A week later, the duo connected for another score, their sixth in three games, as Peyton threw for a Colts' record 404 yards in a 27—19 win at San Diego. "Peyton and I did extra things in the off-season program," said Harrison. "The scramble drill, a lot of patterns, getting our timing down. The work is paying off."

In week seven against the Dallas Cowboys, Peyton and Harrison burned Deion Sanders, one of the league's best defenders, on a wicked play-action fake for a winning 40-yard touchdown. By now, Peyton led the league in yards passing, Harrison in yards receiving, and James in yards rushing. These marks were no fluke. The Colts were working hard. "Peyton prepares like a champion," said lineman Mark Thomas, "and it rubs off."

The Colts beat the Kansas City Chiefs for their fourth win in a row and kept the streak going with wins over the New York Giants, the Philadelphia Eagles, the New York Jets, the Miami Dolphins, the

New England Patriots, the Washington Redskins, and the Cleveland Browns. "Last year we hoped we could win games," Peyton said. "This year we really do believe we can win and that helps you play better."

The Colts finished the season with a 13–3 record—the biggest one-year turnaround in league history—and made the play-offs. Six of the wins were fourth-quarter comebacks, showing that Peyton was cool in the clutch. He also set a new Colts' record with 4,135 passing yards. A play-off loss to the Tennessee Titans spoiled the team's brilliant season. But Indianapolis fans knew their Colts were winners.

Peyton worked tirelessly in the off-season—lifting weights, running sprints, practicing with his receivers, and studying film. He was eager for his third year to start. "You can't just talk about how well things went last year," he said. "That's over with. This is all about today. We're going to set our expectations pretty high."

Peyton was primed to lead another march.

Peyton smiles as the 2000 football season starts.

5

All the Right Moves

The Colts opened the 2000 season in loud Arrowhead Stadium with an easy 27–14 win over the Kansas City Chiefs. After splitting their next four games, including the *Monday Night Football* win against Jacksonville, they reeled off wins over the Seattle Seahawks, the New England Patriots, and the Detroit Lions to reach the season's midpoint at 6–2.

But then the Colts defense began to leak. Opponents scored often. Peyton and his offensive mates tried to keep up, but the team lost four of its next five games to fall to 7–6. Unless the Colts won their last three games, they'd miss the play-offs.

Peyton made it happen. First, the Colts throttled the Buffalo Bills 44–20. Next, they won at Miami, 20–13. Finally, they hammered the Minnesota Vikings, as Peyton threw for a career-high four touchdowns and broke Johnny Unitas's record for touchdown passes in a season. Peyton also became just the fifth quarterback in history to pass for more than 4,000 yards in back-to-back seasons. More important to Peyton, the Colts were in the play-offs again.

Peyton making a move against the Buffalo Bills

Peyton and wide receiver Marvin Harrison

Unfortunately, the team lost 23−17 in the first round against Miami, with the Dolphins scoring in overtime to end the Colts' season. Peyton's response? Strap it on and try again.

A month later, at the 2001 **Pro Bowl** in Hawaii, he completed 16 of 22 passes for 150 yards and two touchdowns, including a perfect 24-yard strike to

Colts teammate Marvin Harrison. He led his AFC teammates to a 38—17 win over the NFC.

In the locker room after the game, Peyton was surrounded by reporters, just as he always is. "[The game] was fun," he said. "I was looking for Marvin a little bit while we were in there together. You kind of know what the other guy can do, so it's an advantage."

Peyton did not boast about his great plays. In fact, he never brags. He is confident, with a firm handshake, yet he is humble and polite. He says, "Yes, sir" and "No, sir" in a soft-spoken voice. "A lot of guys will go out there and try to make people think how tough they are," said his father. "Peyton is not like that. He's very tough, believe me. He just doesn't need to try and let the world know how tough he is."

How tough is he? When a 280-pound defensive lineman plows into him at full speed, that's equal to 2,234 pounds of force. That's like Peyton running head-on (wearing pads) into a brick wall at 21 miles an hour or having a 240-pound refrigerator fall on him from the roof of a house.

Off the field, however, Peyton doesn't act tough. In fact, he is the NFL's "poster boy"—a model player who is friendly and eager to please the fans. He answers his on-line fan mail as much as possible. He signs autographs everywhere he goes and even carries his own pen so he can do so. He seems almost too good to be true.

Not that Peyton is perfect. "He has an amazing grasp of what to do on the field, but he can't do anything else on his own," notes Baldwin Montgomery, one of Peyton's oldest friends. "He's always going to be the guy who steps in dog poop, and every time he eats a sandwich or a hamburger, he'll end up with ketchup down his leg, mustard on his ear."

All laughs aside, there isn't a pro football player more generous than Peyton Manning. Through his PeyBack Foundation, he gives hundreds of thousands of dollars a year to needy kids. He also donates huge sums to food banks, Toys for Tots, the Christmas for Kids campaign, and Boys and Girls Clubs. He runs a program for foster children called Peyton's Pals. He helped write *Peyton's Playbook*, a kid's guide to staying healthy and making good decisions. He also sponsors the annual PeyBack Classic, a football tournament for local schoolchildren held at the RCA Dome.

"I've tried to keep myself out of bad situations, and if that means I'm a Goody Two-shoes, so be it," Peyton says. "In today's world, you see a lot of

Peyton in a tuxedo at the Eighth Annual ESPY Awards for excellence in sports performance

people saying they're not role models, that they don't want to accept that responsibility. I disagree. I have a great opportunity here. Why not reach out and help someone be a good person, resist temptation, and stay in school? I try to be a person that people can look up to. I'm not doing it for any fake reasons. That's the person I want to be. My parents taught me to do the right thing, and that's what I try to do."

Career Highlights

College Statistics

Year	Team	Attempts	Com-pletions	Yards	Per-centage	Touch-downs	Inter-ceptions
1994	Tennessee	144	89	1,141	61.8	11	6
1995	Tennessee	380	244	2,954	64.2	22	4
1996	Tennessee	380	243	3,287	63.9	20	12
1997	Tennessee	477	287	3,819	60.2	36	11

Pro Statistics

Year	Team	Attempts	Com-pletions	Yards	Per-centage	Touch-downs	Inter-ceptions
1998	Indianapolis	575	326	3,739	56.7	26	28
1999	Indianapolis	533	331	4,135	62.1	26	15
2000	Indianapolis	571	357	4,413	62.5	33	15

Glossary

All-American: One of a group of outstanding athletes, chosen each year by news and sports organizations. All-Americans are named in football, baseball, basketball, and other sports, at both the high school and the college levels.

coverage: The formation, or set up, of defensive players at the line of scrimmage before the snap

curl route: A play in which the receiver runs a short distance and then turns with a curling motion to wait for the throw

double-team: To guard an opponent with two players at once

drop back: To step straight back from the line of scrimmage before throwing the ball

endorse: To express support for a company and its products, often by appearing in advertisements

line of scrimmage: An imaginary line on the football field that marks the position of the ball at the start of each down

pass rush: The movement of defenders toward the quarterback

play-action: A play in which the quarterback fakes a handoff before passing the ball

post pattern: A play in which the receiver runs toward a goalpost to receive a pass

Pro Bowl: The yearly all-star game in which teams of players from the NFL's National Football Conference and American Football Conference compete against one another. Fans, coaches, and players vote to choose the game's participants.

snap: The handoff from the center, backward through his legs to the quarterback. The snap puts the ball in play at the start of each down.

turnover: Losing possession of the football due to an error, such as a fumble or an interception

Sources

Information for this book was obtained from the following sources: Paul Attner (*Sporting News*, 12 October 1998); Bill Benner (*Indianapolis Star*, 26 September 2000); Conrad Brunner (*Indianapolis Star*, 18 April 1998; 26 September 2000); Mike Bruton (*Philadelphia Inquirer*, 16 August 2000); Marty Burns (*Sports Illustrated*, 14 September 1998); Mike Chappell (*Football Digest*, September 2000); Nicholas J. Cotsonika (*Detroit Free Press*, 25 August 1998); Joe Frisaro (*Football Digest*, January 1999); Rick Gosselin (*Dallas Morning News*, 18 April 1998, 26 September 2000); Todd Harmonson (*Orange County Register*, 26 September 1999); Mike Kern (*Philadelphia Daily News*, 8 September 1995; 31 December 1997); Peter King (*Sports Illustrated*, 13 April 1998); Terry Lefton (*Brandweek*, 10 August 1998); Douglas S. Looney (*Christian Science Monitor*, 14 August 1998); Steve Lopez (*Time*, 19 October 1998); Ira Miller (*San Francisco Chronicle*, 26 September 2000); Jeff Miller (*Orange County Register*, 31 December 1997); Rick Morrissey (*Chicago Tribune*, 13 December 1997); Charles P. Pierce (*Esquire*, September 1999); Pete Prisco (*Jacksonville Times-Union*, 26 September 2000); Diane Pucin (*Philadelphia Inquirer*, 12 December 1997); Michael Silver (*Sports Illustrated*, 22 November 1999).

Index

Write to Peyton

You can send mail to Peyton at the address on the right. If you write a letter, don't get your hopes up too high. Peyton and other athletes get lots of letters every day, and they aren't always able to answer them all.

Peyton Manning
Indianapolis Colts
7001 West 56th Street
Indianapolis, IN 46254
e-mail: info@colts.com

Acknowledgments

Photographs reproduced with permission of: © Greg Trott/ENDZONE, pp. 1, 11; © Jeff Carlick/ENDZONE, p. 2; © Elsa/ALLSPORT USA, pp. 6, 9; AP/Wide World Photos, p. 14; © Philip Gould/CORBIS, p. 16; © Jamie Squire/ALLSPORT USA, p. 19; © Anders Krusberg/Globe Photos, Inc., pp. 23, 40, 42; Tami Chappell/Reuters/Getty Images, pp. 25, 39; © Jonathan Daniel/ALLSPORT USA, pp. 26, 49; © Rob Tringali Jr./SportsChrome, p. 31; © Al Bello/ALLSPORT USA, p. 32; © Andy Lyons/ALLSPORT USA, p. 33; Winston Luzier/Reuters/Getty Images, p. 37; Brent Smith/Reuters/Getty Images, pp. 44, 47; © Michael Zito/SportsChrome, p. 52; © Vincent Manniello/SportsChrome, p. 54; Jim Bourg/Reuters/Getty Images, p. 55; © Fitzroy Barrett/Globe Photos, Inc., p. 58.
Front cover photograph by © Jeff Carlick/ENDZONE
Back cover photograph by © Jerry Pinkus/SportsChrome

Artwork by Tim Seeley.

About the Author

Jeff Savage is the author of more than 100 sports books, including LernerSports biographies of Sammy Sosa, Jeff Gordon, Julie Foudy, and Kobe Bryant. He and his family live in Napa, California.